Papa Is a Poet

NAT HEAD'S
WOODS

LONDONDERRY TURNPIKE

STONE WALL BOUNDARY

FARM HOUSE

BARN

LITTLE
MOWING
FIELD

ORCHARD

LITTLE
PASTURE

BIG PASTURE

HYLA BROOK

LITTLE
GROVE

SPRING

MERRIAM'S
CELLAR HOLE

GUAY'S
HILL

Natalie S. Bober

Papa Is a Poet

A STORY ABOUT ROBERT FROST

illustrated by Rebecca Gibbon

Christy Ottaviano Books

Henry Holt and Company • New York

It was a cold and gray winter day when our ship docked in New York City. Mama, Papa, my brother, two sisters, and I had sailed on a big ship across the Atlantic Ocean from England to New York City. I am Lesley Frost, and at fifteen I am the oldest child. We were on our way home to New Hampshire after living in England for two years. We returned with little money, and Papa was worried about how he would earn a living.

As we headed uptown to Grand Central Terminal, we stopped at
a newsstand to buy a paper. Mama picked up a copy of the magazine
The New Republic and was startled to discover a review of a book of
poems called *North of Boston,* written by my papa, Robert Frost, and
published by an American publisher.

Papa had been writing poetry in
England. He had two books published
there, but he had not been paid for them
nor had he been told of any specific
arrangements made with an American
publisher. Papa was confused, yet
overjoyed—he had to find out what
was happening!

Papa quickly settled us in Grand
Central Terminal to wait for him and
for the train that would take us home
that night. Then he walked by himself to
the publisher, about fifteen blocks away.

Sitting in the terminal, I began to think back
to our time in New Hampshire before we went
to England. We lived on a farm in Derry that Great-
Grandfather Frost had bought for us. I remembered
picking apples in the orchard, running through the
fields and woodlands, and playing in the pasture
spring that flowed into a little brook named
Hyla Brook.

Papa was a poultry farmer—he raised chickens and sold their eggs. I loved searching for the eggs the hens had laid. I was almost two years old when we moved to the farm from Lawrence, Massachusetts, where I had been born. My brother and sisters were born on the farm.

Sundays were special days.
Sundays meant all-day picnics with
Mama and Papa at Hyla Brook.

Papa had cleared the underbrush with an axe and clippers, and Mama would sit on a board bench that Papa had nailed between two young pine trees. She would mend stockings or read aloud to us. We would build dams, play house using plantain leaves as our dishes, or hunt for mayflowers.

Often we would go for a walk with Papa in search
of wildflowers, then bring our "bokas" to Mama.

We learned the names of all the flowers
and all the birds. When Papa farmed, we trailed
after him, too. At dinner, we shared our stories.

"You ought to have seen what I saw on my way
To the village, through Patterson's pasture today:
Blueberries as big as the end of your thumb. . . ."

We lived too far from town to go to school, so Mama and Papa were our teachers. Studying was called "playing school," and it took place every morning at ten o'clock. Mama taught us to read, to count, to sing, and to tell stories. Papa taught me to use his typewriter when I was three years old. I sounded out the words and spelled them the way I heard them. At four I was beginning to read, and at five I was writing little stories on the typewriter.

When we were a bit older and living in England, we all wrote stories and poems that I typed up. We did small drawings and bound them in heavy paper covers, and named our venture "The Bouquet." I was the editor.

Papa told us that when he was young he had
good friends at school but no friends to play with
who lived close by, and so he sometimes felt like

Some boy too far from town to learn baseball,
Whose only play was what he found himself,
Summer or winter, and could play alone.

Evening time meant a short walk after supper
with Papa to watch the sun go down, hear the
birds sing softly, and smell the soft mist rising
from the meadow.

After our walk we settled in the parlor.
We knew that, as certainly as night followed
day, Mama and Papa would read to us. They
read from books that they loved, passing the
book back and forth between them. We were
allowed to stay and listen until we became
sleepy. Then Mama let us cuddle up and go
to sleep in whichever bed we chose.

Papa thought that any book worth reading twice was worth owning. So instead of buying desserts, we bought books.

Papa told us to reread stories we remembered with pleasure. He wanted us to enjoy books so much that we would be lonely without them. And he told us to memorize poems in order to *know them by heart.*

We were learning to put what we saw and what we felt on paper. Papa told us to describe anything in which we saw humor or beauty. And to look meant to look carefully, to compare, and to bring on what he called "metaphor."

When we asked him what a metaphor was, Papa explained that when a writer names something as something else, he is using metaphor. He is comparing two unlike things that actually have something important in common.

To think to know the country and not know
The hillside on the day the sun lets go
Ten million silver lizards out of snow!

Papa loved words, and he loved Mama.
So it was natural that when he was about
to go off to do a chore on the farm, he
would say to her,

I'm going out to clean the pasture spring;
I'll only stop to rake the leaves away
(And wait to watch the water clear, I may):
I shan't be gone long.—You come too.

And when Mama was expecting a baby, and took a nap every afternoon, Papa would go for a long walk "botanizing," looking for the rare orchid or even rarer fern. Then he would come home with a bunch of flowers for her and apologize:

They are yours, and be the measure
Of their worth for you to treasure,
The measure of the little while
That I've been long away.

Papa loved to study the heavens, and he shared
with us his delight in astronomy. He gave us each a star
to "own." Mine was Arcturus, the brightest star in the
constellation Boötes. Papa had a three-foot-long brass
telescope propped on a window in an upstairs bedroom.
We took turns looking through it. We learned the
constellations by heart. Once he woke me at midnight
to show me Halley's Comet. Papa told us, "When I
was a boy, my mama helped me sell subscriptions to
a magazine in order to win a telescope of my own."

Papa did things *his* way. He decided to milk his cow at midnight so he could stay awake and read Shakespeare and write poems in the hush of a sleeping household. I remember hearing the neighbors talk about the warm glow of the kerosene lamp in the kitchen window.

And I remember one day when I was walking with Papa and we came upon our French-Canadian farmer neighbor, Napoleon Guay. Papa loved to talk, and he also loved to listen. When Mr. Guay told Papa, "Good fences make good neighbors," Papa pointed to the stone wall separating the two farms and replied,

> *My apple trees will never get across*
> *And eat the cones under his pines, I tell him.*

When Papa listened carefully to the speech of all his farmer neighbors, he heard words that had the ring of pure poetry. "The sentence *sound* often says more than the words," he told me. He wanted to make music out of words. Papa could hear the melody in a sentence.

> *He gives his harness bells a shake*
> *To ask if there is some mistake.*

Our days on the farm were ordinary but meaningful. The cupboard was often bare, yet life was filled to the brim, *"and even above the brim,"* as Papa said. So I wondered why we had to leave and go to England. Mama and Papa had talked about going someplace where it wouldn't matter that Papa wrote poems and was a poultry farmer.

But Papa longed to be where he could "lose himself among strangers, to write poetry without further shame to friends and family who had looked on him as a disappointing failure," Mama said.

They decided to sell the farm and use the money to pay for their move. Then they debated between the wild, natural beauty of Vancouver in Canada and England, where Mama wanted to go and live in a cottage with a thatch-covered roof.

I remember the day when we had gathered round the stove in the kitchen, keeping Mama company as she ironed. Suddenly, Papa said, "Let's toss a coin. Heads, England; tails, Vancouver." In that moment our future was determined.

After what seemed like several hours of daydreaming on my part, Papa returned to us in Grand Central Terminal. There was a twinkle in his eyes. "The American publisher has bought my two books of poems—and they will pay me for them!" he told us excitedly.

Poems had been growing inside Papa during the years we had lived on the Derry farm. In England he was able to have those poems published, and now in America, too!

Papa had the courage to trust his own feelings and know what he had to do. He made a reckless choice:

Two roads diverged in a wood, and I—
I took the one less traveled by,
And that has made all the difference.

The "road" Papa took was the road— or life—of a poet. Now the world can hear the beauty of my papa's words.

 # AUTHOR'S NOTE

Robert Frost's lifelong love of the craft of writing is the quality about him that speaks most eloquently to me. It is the deceptive simplicity of his style that is so intriguing. Poetry is beautiful and graceful writing, often having rhythm and rhyme as well as emotional insight. It says the most important things in the simplest way. A poem is "a momentary stay against confusion," Frost told us. It is a "voyage of discovery" that "begins in delight and ends in wisdom." The extraordinary effort and determination Robert Frost put forth to perfect his technique allowed him to create a new and original world of poetic art.

The Frosts sold the Derry Farm in New Hampshire and sailed to England in 1912, where, they hoped, Robert would have the freedom to write his poetry and Elinor could fulfill her wish to "live under thatch." Indeed, Robert Frost never saw New England as clearly as when he was living in old England, and out of these recollections came some of his best-loved poems.

The Frosts remained in England for two and a half years, and returned home to America on February 13, 1915. Here, Lesley tells her story of that day, when she is fifteen years old. Her brother, Carol, is twelve, and her sisters, Irma and Marjorie, are eleven and almost ten, respectively. Another baby, Elinor Bettina, was born in June 1907, but lived just three days. The Frosts had had an older child— Lesley's brother Elliott, who had died suddenly when he was almost four. Lesley was just a nine-month-old baby then, so she doesn't remember him. When she speaks about the farm, she is remembering the time when she was between the ages of six and twelve.

Lesley and her father had a close relationship, and very early on he taught her to read and write. In 1905, when she was not quite six years old, he encouraged her to keep a journal of her "travels and adventures" around and near the farm. She kept the journal until she was ten. Much of what Lesley says in this story has been adapted from that journal and from my biography, *A Restless Spirit: The Story of Robert Frost*, written some years ago for young adult readers.

Robert Frost wrote many poems on the Derry Farm, all of them rooted in its soil. The years from 1905 to 1909 were crucial in his development. It was during this time that he found the literary direction for his entire life.

Years later, Lesley described it: "Finding the New Hampshire farm, finding *on it* what he had

Robert and his sister, Jeanie, around 1879.

Robert Frost as senior class poet and valedictorian, Lawrence (Massachusetts) High School, 1892.

The Derry farmhouse today. Many of Frost's best poems were written here.

come to seek, made it possible for him to say, 'the core of all my writing was probably those free years I had down on the farm a mile or two from Derry Village.'"

Sentence sounds were, for Frost, the most important part of poetry—music arising from the spoken word. He wanted to make "poetry that talked." He loved to talk, he loved to listen, and he loved gossip.

The idealism of their chosen way of life on the Derry Farm and the courage it took to achieve that life were the sources of some of Frost's most beautiful and moving early poems. I would hope that, through my story and Robert Frost's poems, you will come to understand how this storyteller poet became one of the finest voices in American literature.

The Frost family in 1915, after their return from England. Left to right, front row: Marjorie, Carol; middle row: Lesley, Irma; back row: Elinor, Robert.

ROBERT FROST QUOTATIONS

This thatched cottage was the scene of many happy evenings for the Frosts and their new English poet friends.

"I don't write poetry by the day or week, but by the years."

"No tears in the writer, no tears in the reader."

"No surprise for the writer, no surprise for the reader."

"For me the initial delight is in the surprise of remembering something I didn't know I knew."

"We write of things we see and we write in accents we hear."

"When I was young, I was so interested in baseball that my family was afraid I'd waste my life and be a pitcher. Later, they were afraid I'd waste my life and be a poet. They were right."

"A poem is a momentary stay against confusion." It is a "voyage in discovery" that "begins in delight and ends in wisdom. The figure is the same for love."

"We go to school to learn what books to read for the rest of our lives."

The poet in 1938.

POEMS

THE ROAD NOT TAKEN

Two roads diverged in a yellow wood,
And sorry I could not travel both
And be one traveler, long I stood
And looked down one as far as I could
To where it bent in the undergrowth;

Then took the other, as just as fair,
And having perhaps the better claim,
Because it was grassy and wanted wear;
Though as for that, the passing there
Had worn them really about the same,

And both that morning equally lay
In leaves no step had trodden black.
Oh, I kept the first for another day!
Yet knowing how way leads on to way,
I doubted if I should ever come back.

I shall be telling this with a sigh
Somewhere ages and ages hence:
Two roads diverged in a wood, and I—
I took the one less traveled by,
And that has made all the difference.

THE LAST WORD OF A BLUEBIRD

As told to a child

As I went out a Crow
In a low voice said, "Oh,
I was looking for you.
How do you do?
I just came to tell you
To tell Lesley (will you?)
That her little Bluebird
Wanted me to bring word
That the north wind last night
That made the stars bright
And made ice on the trough
Almost made him cough
His tail feathers off.
He just had to fly!
But he sent her Good-by,
And said to be good,
And wear her red hood,
And look for skunk tracks
In the snow with an ax—
And do everything!
And perhaps in the spring
He would come back and sing."

FLOWER-GATHERING

I left you in the morning,
And in the morning glow
You walked a way beside me
To make me sad to go.
Do you know me in the gloaming,
Gaunt and dusty gray with roaming?
Are you dumb because you know me not,
Or dumb because you know?

All for me? And not a question
For the faded flowers gay
That could take me from beside you
For the ages of a day?
They are yours, and be the measure
Of their worth for you to treasure,
The measure of the little while
That I've been long away.

THE PASTURE

I'm going out to clean the pasture spring;
I'll only stop to rake the leaves away
(And wait to watch the water clear, I may):
I shan't be gone long.—You come too.

I'm going out to fetch the little calf
That's standing by the mother. It's so young
It totters when she licks it with her tongue.
I shan't be gone long.—You come too.

A HILLSIDE THAW

To think to know the country and not know
The hillside on the day the sun lets go
Ten million silver lizards out of snow!
As often as I've seen it done before
I can't pretend to tell the way it's done.
It looks as if some magic of the sun
Lifted the rug that bred them on the floor
And the light breaking on them made them run.
But if I thought to stop the wet stampede,
And caught one silver lizard by the tail,
And put my foot on one without avail,
And threw myself wet-elbowed and wet-kneed
In front of twenty others' wriggling speed—
In the confusion of them all aglitter,
And birds that joined in the excited fun
By doubling and redoubling song and twitter—
I have no doubt I'd end by holding none.

It takes the moon for this. The sun's a wizard
By all I tell; but so's the moon a witch.
From the high west she makes a gentle cast
And suddenly, without a jerk or twitch,
She has her spell on every single lizard.
I fancied when I looked at six o'clock
The swarm still ran and scuttled just as fast.
The moon was waiting for her chill effect.
I looked at nine: the swarm was turned to rock
In every lifelike posture of the swarm,
Transfixed on mountain slopes almost erect.
Across each other and side by side they lay.
The spell that so could hold them as they were
Was wrought through trees without a breath of storm
To make a leaf, if there had been one, stir.
It was the moon's: she held them until day,
One lizard at the end of every ray.
The thought of my attempting such a stay!

STOPPING BY WOODS ON A SNOWY EVENING

Whose woods these are I think I know.
His house is in the village, though;
He will not see me stopping here
To watch his woods fill up with snow.

My little horse must think it queer
To stop without a farmhouse near
Between the woods and frozen lake
The darkest evening of the year.

He gives his harness bells a shake
To ask if there is some mistake.
The only other sound's the sweep
Of easy wind and downy flake.

The woods are lovely, dark, and deep,
But I have promises to keep,
And miles to go before I sleep,
And miles to go before I sleep.

DUST OF SNOW

The way a crow
Shook down on me
The dust of snow
From a hemlock tree

Has given my heart
A change of mood
And saved some part
Of a day I had rued.

NOTHING GOLD CAN STAY

Nature's first green is gold,
Her hardest hue to hold.
Her early leaf's a flower;
But only so an hour.
Then leaf subsides to leaf.
So Eden sank to grief,
So dawn goes down to day.
Nothing gold can stay.

BIRCHES

When I see birches bend to left and right
Across the lines of straighter darker trees,
I like to think some boy's been swinging them.
But swinging doesn't bend them down to stay
As ice storms do. Often you must have seen them
Loaded with ice a sunny winter morning
After a rain. They click upon themselves
As the breeze rises, and turn many-colored
As the stir cracks and crazes their enamel.
Soon the sun's warmth makes them shed crystal shells
Shattering and avalanching on the snow crust—
Such heaps of broken glass to sweep away
You'd think the inner dome of heaven had fallen.
They are dragged to the withered bracken by the load,
And they seem not to break; though once they are bowed
So low for long, they never right themselves:
You may see their trunks arching in the woods
Years afterwards, trailing their leaves on the ground
Like girls on hands and knees that throw their hair
Before them over their heads to dry in the sun.
But I was going to say when Truth broke in
With all her matter of fact about the ice storm,
I should prefer to have some boy bend them
As he went out and in to fetch the cows—
Some boy too far from town to learn baseball,
Whose only play was what he found himself,
Summer or winter, and could play alone.
One by one he subdued his father's trees
By riding them down over and over again
Until he took the stiffness out of them,

And not one but hung limp, not one was left
For him to conquer. He learned all there was
To learn about not launching out too soon
And so not carrying the tree away
Clear to the ground. He always kept his poise
To the top branches, climbing carefully
With the same pains you use to fill a cup
Up to the brim, and even above the brim.
Then he flung outward, feet first, with a swish,
Kicking his way down through the air to the ground.
So was I once myself a swinger of birches.
And so I dream of going back to be.
It's when I'm weary of considerations,
And life is too much like a pathless wood
Where your face burns and tickles with the cobwebs
Broken across it, and one eye is weeping
From a twig's having lashed across it open.
I'd like to get away from earth awhile
And then come back to it and begin over.
May no fate willfully misunderstand me
And half grant what I wish and snatch me away
Not to return. Earth's the right place for love:
I don't know where it's likely to go better.
I'd like to go by climbing a birch tree,
And climb black branches up a snow-white trunk
Toward heaven, till the tree could bear no more,
But dipped its top and set me down again.
That would be good both going and coming back.
One could do worse than be a swinger of birches.

OCTOBER

O hushed October morning mild,
Thy leaves have ripened to the fall;
Tomorrow's wind, if it be wild,
Should waste them all.
The crows above the forest call;
Tomorrow they may form and go.
O hushed October morning mild,
Begin the hours of this day slow.
Make the day seem to us less brief.
Hearts not averse to being beguiled,
Beguile us in the way you know.
Release one leaf at break of day;
At noon release another leaf;
One from our trees, one far away.
Retard the sun with gentle mist;
Enchant the land with amethyst.
Slow, slow!
For the grapes' sake, if they were all,
Whose leaves already are burnt with frost,
Whose clustered fruit must else be lost—
For the grapes' sake along the wall.

THE RUNAWAY

Once when the snow of the year was beginning to fall,
We stopped by a mountain pasture to say,
 "Whose colt?"
A little Morgan had one forefoot on the wall,
The other curled at his breast. He dipped his head
And snorted at us. And then he had to bolt.
We heard the miniature thunder where he fled,
And we saw him, or thought we saw him, dim
 and gray,
Like a shadow against the curtain of falling flakes.
"I think the little fellow's afraid of the snow.
He isn't winter-broken. It isn't play
With the little fellow at all. He's running away.
I doubt if even his mother could tell him, 'Sakes,
It's only weather.' He'd think she didn't know!
Where is his mother? He can't be out alone."
And now he comes again with clatter of stone,
And mounts the wall again with whited eyes
And all his tail that isn't hair up straight.
He shudders his coat as if to throw off flies.
"Whoever it is that leaves him out so late,
When other creatures have gone to stall and bin,
Ought to be told to come and take him in."

MENDING WALL

Something there is that doesn't love a wall,
That sends the frozen-ground-swell under it
And spills the upper boulders in the sun,
And makes gaps even two can pass abreast.
The work of hunters is another thing:
I have come after them and made repair
Where they have left not one stone on a stone,
But they would have the rabbit out of hiding,
To please the yelping dogs. The gaps I mean,
No one has seen them made or heard them made,
But at spring mending-time we find them there.
I let my neighbor know beyond the hill;
And on a day we meet to walk the line
And set the wall between us once again.
We keep the wall between us as we go.
To each the boulders that have fallen to each.
And some are loaves and some so nearly balls
We have to use a spell to make them balance:
"Stay where you are until our backs are turned!"
We wear our fingers rough with handling them.
Oh, just another kind of outdoor game,
One on a side. It comes to little more:
There where it is we do not need the wall:

He is all pine and I am apple orchard.
My apple trees will never get across
And eat the cones under his pines, I tell him.
He only says, "Good fences make good neighbors."
Spring is the mischief in me, and I wonder
If I could put a notion in his head:
"*Why* do they make good neighbors? Isn't it
Where there are cows? But here there are no cows.
Before I built a wall I'd ask to know
What I was walling in or walling out,
And to whom I was like to give offense.
Something there is that doesn't love a wall,
That wants it down." I could say "Elves" to him,
But it's not elves exactly, and I'd rather
He said it for himself. I see him there,
Bringing a stone grasped firmly by the top
In each hand, like an old-stone savage armed.
He moves in darkness as it seems to me,
Not of woods only and the shade of trees.
He will not go behind his father's saying,
And he likes having thought of it so well
He says again, "Good fences make good neighbors."

For my great-grandchildren, with love:

Sam, Emily, and Hannah,

Brianna, Gabbi, and Levi,

and Sydney —N. S. B.

For my parents

and all those who took the

road less traveled —R. G.

BIBLIOGRAPHY

Barry, Elaine. *Robert Frost on Writing*. New Brunswick, NJ: Rutgers University Press, 1973.

Bober, Natalie S. *A Restless Spirit: The Story of Robert Frost*. New York: Henry Holt and Company, 1991.

Evans, William R. *Robert Frost and Sidney Cox: Forty Years of Friendship*. Hanover, NH: University Press of New England, 1981.

Frost, Lesley. *New Hampshire's Child: The Derry Journals of Lesley Frost*. Albany, NY: State University of New York Press, 1969.

Lathem, Edward Connery, Editor. *The Poetry of Robert Frost*. New York: Holt, Rinehart and Winston, 1969.

Walsh, John Evangelist. *Into My Own: The English Years of Robert Frost*. New York: Grove Press, 1988.

Henry Holt and Company, LLC, *Publishers since 1866*
175 Fifth Avenue, New York, New York 10010
mackids.com

Henry Holt® is a registered trademark of Henry Holt and Company, LLC.
Text copyright © 2013 by Natalie S. Bober
Illustrations copyright © 2013 by Rebecca Gibbon
All rights reserved.

Library of Congress Cataloging-in-Publication Data
Bober, Natalie.
Papa is a poet : a story about Robert Frost / Natalie S. Bober ;
illustrated by Rebecca Gibbon.
        pages   cm
Summary: "When Robert Frost was a child, his family thought he would grow
up to be a baseball player. Instead, he became a poet. His life on a farm in
New Hampshire inspired him to write 'poetry that talked,' and today he is
famous for his vivid descriptions of the rural life he loved so much. There was
a time, though, when Frost had to struggle to get his poetry published. Told
from the point of view of Lesley, Robert Frost's oldest daughter, this is the story
of how a lover of language found his voice" —Provided by publisher.
Includes bibliographical references.
ISBN 978-0-8050-9407-7 (hardback)
1. Frost, Robert, 1874–1963–Juvenile literature. 2. Poets, American–20th century–
Biography–Juvenile literature. I. Gibbon, Rebecca, illustrator. II. Title.
PS3511.R94Z5547 2013   811'.52–dc23   [B]   2013005350

First Edition—2013 / Designed by April Ward
The artist used acrylic ink, colored pencil, and watercolor on
acid-free cartridge paper to create the illustrations for this book.

Permission to reprint the following copyrighted material is gratefully acknowledged:
"The Road Not Taken," "The Last Word of a Bluebird," "Flower-Gathering," "The Pasture,"
"Stopping by Woods on a Snowy Evening," "A Hillside Thaw," "Dust of Snow," "Nothing
Gold Can Stay," "Birches," "October," "Mending Wall," "The Runaway," and "Blueberries"
from the book *The Poetry of Robert Frost* edited by Edward Connery Lathem. Copyright
© 1916, 1923, 1930, 1934, 1939, 1967, 1969 by Henry Holt and Company, copyright
© 1944, 1951, 1958, 1962 by Robert Frost, copyright © 1967 by Lesley Frost Ballantine.
Reprinted by permission of Henry Holt and Company, LLC.

    Photos in the author's note are courtesy of the following:
[Frost with his sister and the thatched house] Courtesy of Dartmouth College Library;
[Frost family in NH in 1915] George H. Browne Robert Frost Collection, Michael J.
Spinelli, Jr. Center for University Archives and Special Collections, Herbert H. Lamson
Library and Learning Commons, Plymouth State University; [Frost as valedictorian,
Lawrence High School, 1892 and Frost as an older man sitting against a tree] Courtesy of
the Jones Library, Inc., Amherst, Massachusetts.

Printed in China by South China Printing Co. Ltd., Dongguan City, Guangdong Province.

10 9 8 7 6 5 4 3 2 1